D0170161

Best
Brain Teasers
For Kids

Peter MacDonald

ISBN-13:
978-1500529994

ISBN-10:
1500529990

LETS HAVE SOME FUN

CONTENTS

Contents

PETER MACDONALD

Best Joke Book for Kids Series

http://www.amazon.com/dp/B00EKVOG28

http://www.amazon.com/dp/B00ETYQWGE

http://www.amazon.com/dp/B00FA2A8PU

x

x

2

Best Brain Teasers for Kids

Brain teasers are word puzzles that may be spoken or written and they require you to use mental reasoning to find the answer to the puzzle. Generally, you only need your brain to solve these puzzles.

Basically, using brain teasers is like doing a workout specifically for your brain. The more you work your brain, the stronger and more developed it becomes.

Benefits of Brain Teasers

Brain teasers offer a number of benefits, especially for children. Studies show that playing mind games, such as brain teasers, can increase blood flow to the brain, increasing the performance of the brain.

The increase in blood flow also results in important chemical changes that result in improved brain function.

Using brain teasers regularly offers a fun way that children can improve cognitive skills, such as comprehension, memory, attention, perception, language skills and more. Brain teasers help to improve alertness and concentration in children. They help to activate the thinking process, exercising and stimulating the mind.

Since brain teasers are fun and exciting, children can have a great time while exercising their brain and developing improved mental skills.

Brain teasers are fun to do alone, or they can be done as a team to encouraging working together.

Some children even enjoy competing against friends to see who is able to figure out the right answer first.

Easy Brain Teasers

Starting out with easy brain teasers is a great way to begin getting your brain in shape. Easy brain teasers help warm up the brain, training your brain and making it stronger.

Start working on these simple brain teasers before you move on to harder ones. Once you find it easy to solve the easy brain teasers, then you can go on to moderately hard teasers, working your way up to difficult ones.

The following are some easy brain teasers to get you started.

1 – An electric train is traveling north. The wind is blowing from the south-west. Which way is the smoke from the train blowing?

2 – Sam, Kevin, Nick, Henry and Brian were all taking a walk around a big lake while they were on vacation during the rainy season.

Brian was wearing a waterproof cap and a raincoat.

Henry and Kevin both were comfortable with the umbrellas they were carrying. Henry gave his umbrella to Sam.

However, no one gave poor Nick anything to protect himself from the rain. However, Nick did not get wet. How is this possible?

3 – How is it possible to make libraries bigger without building anything?

4 – What animals have the best education?

5 – What is unable to run, even though it has three feet?

6 – How can you make an egg roll?

7 – If five dollars are on the table and I take three dollars away, how many dollars will I have?

8 – Penguins can move as fast as five miles per hour. How long will it take a penguin to fly 80 miles?

9 – A father and son were driving and they ended up in a car accident.

They were taken to two separate hospitals.

The son was ready for an operation when the surgeon suddenly said, "I cannot operate on him. He is my son!"

Who was the surgeon?

10 – A barrel is filled with water and it weighs 120 pounds. A man puts something into the barrel and now weighs less than 120 pounds. What did the man put in the barrel?

11 – Jimmy has two U.S coins. The two coins total fifty-five cents. One is not a nickel. What coins does Jimmy have?

12 – Farmer Dan had 10 sheep. All but eight died.

How many sheep does farmer Dan have left?

13 – Some months have as many as 31 days while others have 30 days.

How many months have 28 days?

14 – What word is always spelled wrong?

15 – Eight children were walking to the bookstore.

All but two decided to stop at the ice cream parlor instead.

How many children made it to the bookstore?

16 – Two men are playing checkers.

They each play seven complete games.

Both men win the same number of checkers games. No ties occur.

How is this possible?

17 – You are running a marathon.

As you are running, you finally overtake the person who is in 2nd place.

What place are you currently in?

18 – A rooster is laying eggs on the rooftop.

Which way do those eggs roll?

19 – A fire broke out in a 15 story building.

A woman gets scared and panics, jumping out of the window to escape the fire.

She survives. How?

20 – You can catch it but you cannot throw it. What is it?

21 – When you take my skin off, I do not cry. However, you may cry. What am I?

22 – Which word does not belong in this group?

First, Second, Third, Forth, Fifth, Sixth, Seventh, Eighth, Ninth

23 – My top and bottom both have holes.
I have holes in the middle and on the sides
too. However, I can still hold water.

Can you guess what I am?

Moderately Hard Brain Teasers

Once you have mastered easy brain teasers, it's time to start challenging your brain a bit more.

Enjoy a tougher challenge by trying out these moderately hard brain teasers.

1 – You have one match. You walk into a room and you have a wood burning stove, an oil burner and an oil lamp.

What do you light first?

2 – On a winter day, a pure white dog crosses the street.

It has been storming for hours and no one has plowed the road. People can easily see the dog. How?

3 – Henry grows cherries and decides to sell them at a local farmer's market.

He plans to charge $2.50 for each basket of cherries.

The first day he sells 15 baskets of cherries. The second day he only sells 12. The third day he has a great day and sells 35. The fourth day is rainy and he only sells 3. The fifth day he sells 10. The sixth day he sells 18. Then, on the seventh day, he sells 22 and three quarters.

How many baskets of strawberries does he sell in seven days?

4 – A cyclist crosses the French and Spanish border every single day.

He always carries a bag. However, no matter how many times he is searched and investigated, they cannot figure out what he's smuggling.

Can you figure out what he is smuggling?

5 – A man is captive in an island prison.

He does not know how to swim.

Finally, he escapes from the prison and has nothing but himself.

There is not a bridge to help him.

How did the man escape from the prison?

6 – A woman was speeding and she ran right through a stop sign.

There were two police officers that saw it happen but they simply sat there and did nothing.

Why?

7 – Pinkie Pinkerton was living in a beautiful, pink, one story home that was located on Pink Street.

The roof, the carpet, the pictures, the furniture, the walls, the bathroom, the yard and the flowers were all pink.

Everything in the house was pink.

What color was the stairway in her house?

8 – Jane walked all day long. At the end of the day, she had only move two feet.

How can this be?

9 – What can move backwards and forwards, yet it has no legs.

It is not able to talk, walk, crawl or slither. It comes in all colors, shapes and sizes.

What is it?

10 – You go into a bathroom that has no windows and stone walls.

You start to run a bath but the handles break off and you have no way to turn off the tap.

Since the door is locked on the outside and no windows are in the bathroom, you cannot escape.

The room will soon flood and you will end up drowning.

Is there a way that you can save yourself?

11 – A baseball game ends and the score is 6 to 3.
No walks occurred and no one stole any bases. No men score runs.

How could this be?

12 – Five boys were in a foot race.

Mark finished before Sam, but behind Ed. Ron finished before John, but behind Sam.

In what order did all the boys end up finishing the foot race?

13 – Jenny loves cats and has several as pets.

All but two cats are totally black. All but two are totally white. All but two happen to be completely ginger.

How many cats does Jenny have?

14 – The school orchestra has 21 musicians and they can complete Beethoven's Moonlight Sonata in just 5 minutes and 31 seconds.

If the school orchestra doubled the number of musicians, how long would it take for the orchestra to play the piece of music?

15 – I always run and I never walk. While I have a bed, I never sleep.

Even though I have a mouth, I can't eat.

What am I?

16 – I will follow you all through the day.

When rain or night comes, I disappear.

What am I?

17 – An old cowboy rides into a small city on Friday.

The cowboy stays in the city two days and he leaves the city on Saturday.

How is this possible?

18 – I belong to you, but other people use it a lot more than you use it.

What am I?

19 – Three houses are located in a row. One house is blue, one house is white and one house is red.

The blue house is to the right of the middle house. The red house is to the left of the middle house.

Where is the white house?

20 – In a dictionary, you will always find one work that is spelled incorrectly.

What word is it?

21 – All day long I run around over fields, streets, woods and more.

When I sit under the bed at night, I am never alone.

My tongue hangs out as I wait to be filled again in the morning.

What am I?

22 – Jane's mother has four kids.

The first child is named April, the second child is named May and the third child is named June.

What did the mother name her fourth child?

23 – You are driving a big city bus.

Five people get on and two people get off the bus.

Then, at the next stop, ten people get on the bus and 12 get off the bus.

Next, three people get off the bus and 5 people get on the bus.

Can you figure out the color of the bus driver's eyes?

24 – In Colorado, it snows 44 inches.

While you have two snow blowers, you do not have fuel for them.

Your next door neighbor living in San Francisco does have some fuel, but you do not like to talk to him.

What can you do?

25 – The Mississippi River lies right between Arkansas and Tennessee, dividing the two states.

If a plane ends up crashing right in the middle of the river, where will the survivors end up being buried?

Difficult Brain Teasers

1 – Put a coin into an empty bottle.

Then, place a cork into the bottle's neck.

Can you figure out a way to take the coin out of the bottle without breaking the bottle or taking the cork out of the bottle?

2 – A farmer comes to a river and has a fox, chicken and a bag of grain with him.

He has a boat to help get them across the river but it only will hold one other thing besides him.

However, as he takes the items across, he cannot leave the chicken and the fox together, since the fox will eat the chicken.

He cannot leave the chicken and the grain together because the chicken will eat the grain. How does the farmer manage to get all of the items across safely?

3 – Look at this paragraph. Can you find out what is unusual about it? It looks plain and you probably think nothing is wrong. Nothing is wrong with it, but it is unusual. Study it thoroughly and think. You may not find anything that is odd about it. Think about for a bit and you may find out what is unusual about this paragraph.

4 – As an old man started getting older, he decided that he wanted to leave his fortune to one of his sons.

He had three sons but he could not figure out which son he should give the fortune to.

To figure it out, he decided to give each son a little money, telling his sons they should buy something that will completely fill the living room.

The first son purchased straw, but the straw could not fill the room. The second son purchased some sticks, but they did not fill the entire room either.

The third son purchase two things and they filled the entire room, and so his father game the third son his fortune.

What did the third son buy and what filled the room?

5 – A ship is anchored within a port and it has a ladder that is hanging over the side.

The very bottom rung is touching the water.

There are six inches between each rung. The ladder is 60 inches in length.

The tide continues to rise at about five inches per hour.

At what point will the water rise enough to reach the fifth rung from the top?

6 – A young lady has been browsing for a long time. Finally, she walks up to the man behind the counter and hands the man a book.

The man looks at the inside tag and says, "That will be $3.50 please." The woman hands the man the money and then walks away, leaving the book behind.

Even though the man sees her leave without the book, he does not try to stop her. Why not?

7 – I have two arms, but fingers none. I have two feet, but cannot run. I carry well, but I have found I carry best with my feet off the ground. What am I?

8 – Pauls height is 6 feet, he's an assistant at a butchers shop, and he wears size 9 shoes.

What does he weigh?

9 – The person who makes it has no need for it.

The person who purchases it does not use it.

The person who does use it does not know he or she is.

What is it?

10 – Complete this sequence of letters: o, t, t, f, f, s, s, _, _, _.

11 – If your sock drawer has 6 black socks, 4 brown socks, 8 white socks, and 2 tan socks, how many socks would you have to pull out in the dark to be sure you had a matching pair?

12 – Torn Suit A man was just doing his job when his suit was torn. Three minutes late he died. Why

13 −

8809 = 6

7111 = 0

2172 = 0

6666 = 4

1111 = 0

3213 = 0

7662 = 2

9312 = 1

0000 = 4

2222 = 0

3333 = 0
5555 = 0

8193 = 3

8096 = 5

7777 = 0

9999 = 4

7756 = 1

6855 = 3

9881 = 5

5531 = 0

2581 = ?

14 –A fast food restaurant sells chicken in orders of 6, 9, and 20.

What is the largest number of pieces of chicken you cannot order from this restaurant?

15 – A woman shoots her husband.

Then she holds him under water for over 5 minutes.

Finally, she hangs him.

But 5 minutes later they both go out together and enjoy a wonderful dinner together.

How can this be?

16 – A man walks into a pub and simply orders a water.

The bar tender simply looks at the man, grabs a shotgun, and points it at the man's face.

The man says, "Thank you" gets up, and walks out of the pub.

Why did they behave this way?

17 – Why can't Kevin Smith, who is now living in Canada, not be buried in the USA?

18– Which creature walks on four legs in the morning, two legs in the afternoon, and three legs in the evening?

19 –Who spends the day at the window, goes to the table for meals and hides at night?

20 – A man is pushing his car along the road when he comes to a hotel. He shouts, "I'm bankrupt!"

Why?

Brain Teaser Answer Key:

Easy Brain Teaser Answers:

1 – There is no smoke because it is an electric train.

2 – It was not raining when Sam, Kevin, Nick, Henry and Brian were walking around the lake.

3 – Add more stories to the library.

4 – Fish. Fish travel in schools.

5 – A yard stick.

6 – Push the egg.

7 – Three dollars, because two dollars are left on the table.

8 – Penguins are not able to fly.

9 – The surgeon was the boy's mother.

10 – The man put a hole in the barrel, letting the water drain out so the barrel weighed less.

11 – Jimmy has a half dollar and a nickel. Remember, it says that only ONE wasn't a nickel.

12 – Farmer Dan has eight sheep left.

13 – All months have 28 days.

14 – The word "wrong."

15 – Two children made it to the library.

16 – The men are not playing checkers against each other.

17 – You are in second place.

18 – Roosters cannot lay eggs.

19 – She jumps out of a window on the first floor of the building.

20 – It is a cold.

21 – I am an onion.

22 – Forth. It is spelled incorrectly for this group and should actually be spelled "fourth."

23 – I am a sponge.

Moderately Hard Brain Teaser

Answers:

1 – You light the match first before you can light anything else.

2 – It's raining not snowing.

3 – None. Henry was selling cherries, not strawberries.

4 – He is smuggling bicycles across the border.

5 – The many escaped prison during the winter. The ice froze and he was able to walk away on the ice.

6 – The woman was running, not driving a car.

7 – There was not a stairway – it is a one story house.

8 – Jane only has two feet, so she only moved two feet while walking.

9 – It is a door.

10 – All you have to do is pull the plug on the bathtub so the water will drain out.

11 – The baseball game was played by all women.

12 – Ed finished first. Mark finished second. Sam finished third. Ron finished fourth. John finished fifth.

13 – Jenny has three cats. One is black, one is white and one is ginger.

14 – The same amount of time. The length of the music piece does not change just because you add more musicians.

15 – I am a river.

16 – I am your shadow.

17 – The name of the cowboy's horse is Friday.

18 – I am your name.

19 – The White House is in Washington, DC.

20 – The word is "Incorrectly."

21 – I am a shoe.

22 – Jane.

23 – What color are your eyes? Remember, YOU are the one who is driving the bus.

24 – You do nothing. Since your neighbor lives in San Francisco, obviously you live there too. You do not need to worry about how much snow is in Colorado.

25 – Nowhere. You do not bury the survivors.

Difficult Brain Teaser Answers:

1 – Yes. You can push the cork until it falls into the bottle and then shake the bottle until the coin falls out.

2 – First, the farmer has to take the chicken to the other side, leaving the grain and fox.

Then, he goes back for the fox, drops it off and takes the chicken with him.

He takes the chicken back, picks the grain up and leaves the chicken behind.

He drops the grain off and leaves it with the fox.

He heads back and gets the chicken, heading to the other side.

They now are all on the same side of the river.

3 – The most common letter in the alphabet, the letter "E," is not used in the entire paragraph.

4 – The third son purchased a candle and a match.

He used the match to light the candle. Light filled the entire room.

5 – If the tide starts rising, the ship continues to rise on the water.

This means that the water will still only be touching the first rung and will never actually touch the fifth rung from the top.

6 – It is a library and the young lady simply paid a fine for a book that was overdue.

7 – A wheel Barrow

8 – He weighs Meat

9 – A coffin.

10 – e, n, t - The first letter of the numbers from one to ten.

11 – Five. There are only four colors, so five socks guarantee t`hat two will be the same color.

12 – He was an astronaut on a space walk, doing repairs.

13 – 2581 = 2

14 – Answer: 43.

After 6 all numbers divisible by 3 can be ordered (because they can all be expressed as a sum of 6's and 9's). After 26, all numbers divisible by three when subtracted by 20 can be obtained. After 46, all numbers divisible by three when subtracted by 40 can be obtained. After 46, all numbers fit into one of these 3 categories, so all numbers can be obtained. 43 is the last number that doesn't fall into one of these categories ($44 = 20 + 6 * 4$, $45 = 6 * 6 + 9$).

15 – She shot a photo of him, developed the print, and hung it up to dry.

16 – The Man had the hiccup and the bar man gave him a fright to cure him.

17 – He is alive

18 – Man. He crawls on all fours as a baby, then walks on two feet as an adult, and then walks with a cane as an old man.

19 – A fly.

20 – He was Playing Monopoly

About the Author

Peter MacDonald loves a good laugh, especially ones he can share with his children. He is committed to creating good clean fun in His series of joke books, "Best Joke Books For Kids". Peter is an Aussie with a good sense of Humor and he enjoys the good things in life, especially his church and family.

Made in the USA
San Bernardino, CA
28 June 2018